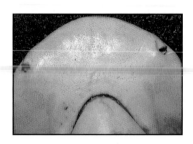

Published by Creative Education
123 South Broad Street, Mankato, Minnesota 56001
Creative Education is an imprint of The Creative Company

Designed by Stephanie Blumenthal

Photographs by Robert Barber, Daniel Gotshall, Innerspace Visions
(Gary Bell, Mark Conlin, A. & A. Ferrari, Chris Newbert, Doug Perrine, Mark Strickland),
Carl Roessler, Tom Stack & Associates (David Fleetham, Thomas Kitchin,
Randy Morse, Brian Parker, Ed Robinson, Mark Stack, Tom Stack),
Norbert Wu Productions (Marjorie Bank, Norbert Wu)

Library of Congress Cataloging-in-Publication Data

Pope, Deidre.
Sharks / Deidre Pope.
p. cm. — (Let's investigate)
Includes index.
ISBN 1-58341-193-3
1. Sharks—Juvenile literature. [1. Sharks.] I. Title. II. Series.
QL638.9 .P59   2001
597.3—dc21   00-064475

First edition

2 4 6 8 9 7 5 3 1

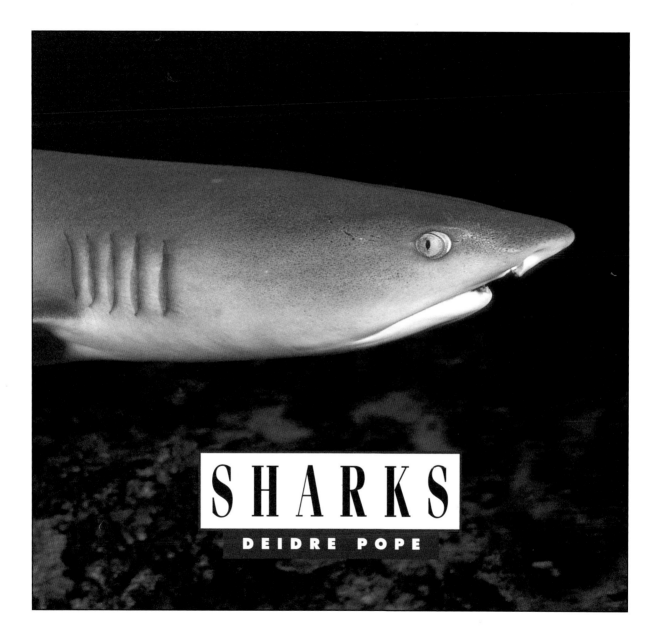

SHARKS
DEIDRE POPE

Creative Education

SHARK

THREAT

A person is more likely to win the lottery or die in an automobile accident than to be attacked by a shark. In fact, bee stings kill more people every year in the United States alone than do sharks.

Above, a sandbar shark Right, a great white shark near Australia

When we think of sharks, we usually think of aggressive creatures that hunt and kill anything including humans—at will. The shark we picture is huge and sinister, ready to leap out of the water and gobble up helpless people sitting on a dock or in a fishing boat. Yet nothing could be further from the truth about the shy, solitary shark. Sharks are not the bloodthirsty monsters humans have made them out to be, but fascinating animals that are superbly **adapted** to their marine habitat.

SHARK

GIANT

Whale sharks are the largest fish in the world. They can grow to be 40 feet (12 m) long and can weigh 13 tons (11.8 t).

SHARK

DWARF

The smallest shark is the dwarf lantern shark, which grows to be only six inches (15 cm) in length.

A blue-spotted fantail ray gliding across the ocean floor

6

SPECIAL KIND OF FISH

The ocean holds more than 400 **species** of sharks. Some of them look like the one we're familiar with—sleek and torpedo-shaped, displaying lots of sharp, jagged teeth. But some are flat as a pancake and glide along the ocean floor. Still others are covered with spots that make them glow blue or green.

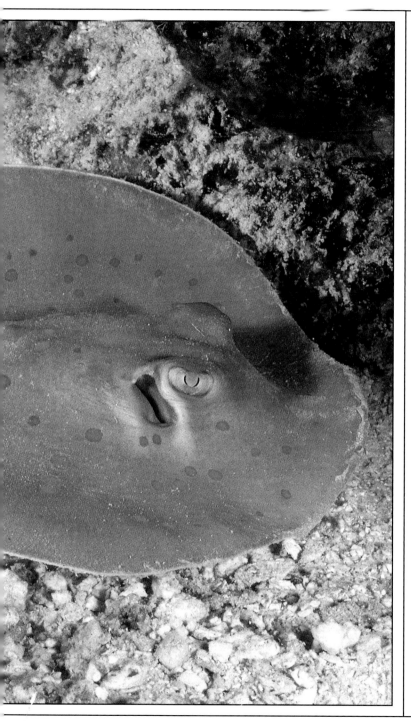

These unique fish belong to a group called *Chondrichthyes* (kon-DRICK-thees), which means they have skeletons made of **cartilage**, not bone like most fish. They can live in temperate (cool) or tropical seas, and some can even live in freshwater. Sharks are found at all depths of the ocean—from shallow coastal areas to the very bottom of the sea.

SHARK
HABITAT

Although most sharks live in the ocean, some, such as the bull shark, can live in freshwater. Bull sharks have been found 1,700 miles (2,735 km) up the Mississippi River.

Above, a bull shark

Unlike bony fish, which have a special swim bladder that fills with gas to keep them afloat, sharks have a very large liver, which is full of oil. Since oil is lighter than water, it makes the liver act like a float, keeping the shark from sinking.

Sharks also have unique skin. Even though it looks smooth, a shark's skin is rough. It is covered with plate-like scales called dermal denticles. The scales are a lot like shark—or human—teeth. Denticles help make the shark **streamlined** as it moves through the water, and they also protect the shark from larger **predators**.

The thresher shark has a narrow tail that is as long as its body. It uses its tail not only to swim, but also to stun its prey.

*Above, a thresher shark
Left, the eye and skin of
a nurse shark
Far left, a Caribbean
reef shark*

SHARK
GLOW

10

*Some deep-water sharks have luminous organs called photopores in their skin that give off light. Scientists think this helps the sharks attract **prey**.*

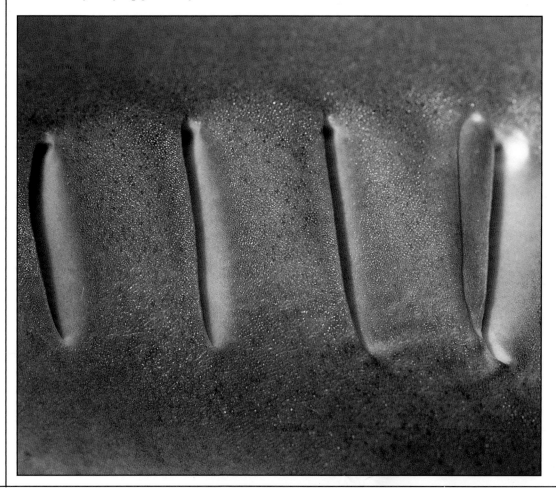

Above, a deep-sea cat shark
Right, the gills of a nurse shark

SHARK BODIES

Sharks use their gills to breathe. As a shark swims, water goes into its mouth and enters an opening that leads to its gills. The shark extracts oxygen from the water and pushes what's left back out of its gills and into the ocean. Many sharks need to move all the time in order to breathe, but a few species have a muscle called a gill pump that constantly pushes water through their gills, even if they're lying perfectly still on the ocean bottom.

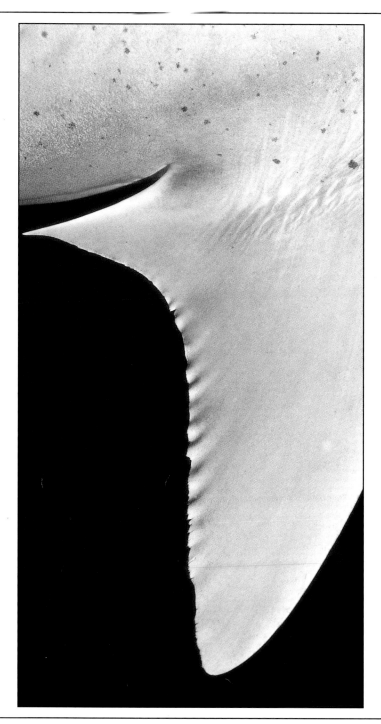

When a shark wants to move, it uses its body, fins, and tail to propel itself through the water. By curving its entire body from side to side, a shark can meander slowly in search of prey or it can accelerate to great speeds. The shark's side fins help it to steer, brake, and hover, while its dorsal fin, the one on its back, helps keep it upright. The shark's tail fins add power for bursts of speed or delicate maneuvering when the shark chases down its next meal.

SHARK
SPEED

Great white sharks normally cruise the ocean at just under two miles (3 km) per hour. When closing in on a kill, however, they can accelerate to 15 miles (24 km) per hour.

A bonnethead shark's side, or pectoral, fin

SHARK
JAWS

Sharks use their teeth and jaws for eating, defense, and social interactions such as mating and courtship.

Teeth rows of the lemon shark

TEETH AND FEEDING

The teeth found in a shark's mouth one day aren't the same teeth the shark had a month earlier. Sharks lose their teeth throughout their lifetimes. Fortunately for the shark, several rows of replacement teeth behind the ones in front are waiting to slide forward and fill in for the ones that get worn out or lost. A shark's teeth are embedded in its gums, not attached to its jaw, making them easily replaced.

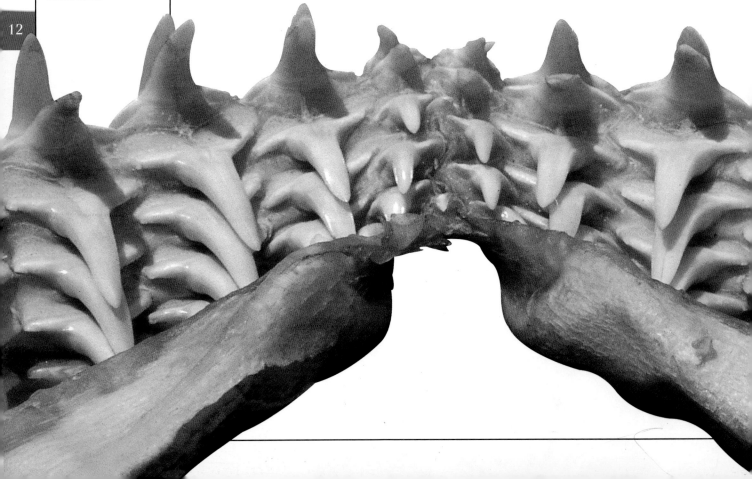

The shape of a shark's teeth varies from species to species and helps determine what the shark eats. Sharks that feed on shellfish have flat, blunt teeth for crushing shells, while those that eat mostly bony fish have small, spike-like teeth for gripping their prey. Filter feeders, such as basking and whale sharks, eat only what enters their mouths with the water they take in. Instead of teeth, these sharks have gill rakers, which look like combs and trap the food that comes into the sharks' mouths.

SHARK

FEEDING

Cookiecutter sharks have round mouths with lots of jagged teeth. They feed by suctioning onto seals, dolphins, and other prey and biting a round plug of flesh from the animals.

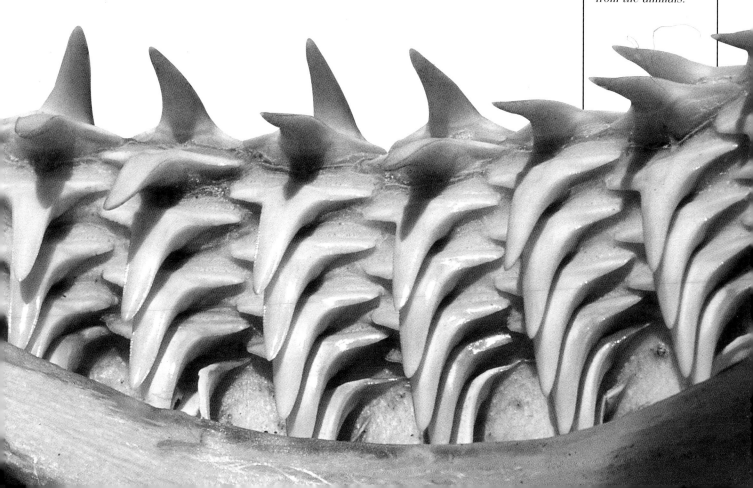

SHARK
FOOD

Some sharks are picky eaters and stick to one kind of food. The whiskery shark, which lives around the rocky reefs off the south coast of Australia, feeds almost exclusively on octopuses.

Sharks normally eat only what they need in order to grow and function. For some sharks, that means they feed once or twice a week; others may go up to a month without food. All sharks are carnivorous (meat-eaters), but different species have different ways of hunting.

An ornate wobbegong shark blending in with its surroundings

Sharks that live on the ocean floor have skin colors and patterns that help them blend in with the sand and vegetation around them. They are so well camouflaged that they can ambush their prey. This means that they hide and wait for their meal to come to them. Angel sharks, for example, cover themselves with sand and wait for their lunch to pass by.

SHARK

CAMOUFLAGE

Wobbegong sharks are flat and have tassels around their head and mouth that make them look like the plants on the ocean floor. Their coloring allows them to blend in with rocks and seaweed.

15

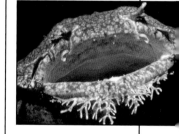

Above, protrusions on the tasselled wobbegong shark resemble plants

SHARK
HUNTING

Spinner sharks enter schools of fish to hunt. They are named for their habit of spinning in circles to confuse their prey.

The more aggressive sharks pursue their prey, using their teeth and powerful jaws to disable it. Once the prey is wounded, the shark waits, then comes back to eat it after it has died. Scientists think that sharks do this in order to avoid being injured by large prey animals, such as sea lions.

A gray shark looking for food

SHARK
DIET

18

Scavenging tiger sharks are often called "the garbage cans of the sea." Researchers have found plastic bags, coal, cans, wood, wire, pets, and live-stock in the bellies of tiger sharks.

While other sharks hide or stalk, filter feeders simply open their mouths and allow **plankton** and small fish to swim in on their own. Some sharks, such as the tiger shark, are scavengers. This means they eat what they find lying around rather than hunt. These sharks help keep the ocean water clear of dead and decaying animals.

Some sharks have learned to follow fishing boats when they are hungry, and many shark species **migrate** in order to find food. Sharks also migrate when they are ready to reproduce.

Above, a tiger shark
Right, a whale shark, the largest fish in the world

SHARK

Basking sharks feed at the surface of the water and sometimes feed together in rows. Early sailors, seeing rows of evenly spaced fins, may have mistaken these sharks for monstrous sea serpents.

19

A great white shark taking bait set by photographers

SHARK

MATING

Mature male sharks mate every season, but mature females mate only every second or third season.

SHARK

SKIN

Female sharks usually have thicker skins than males. Researchers think this might be nature's way of protecting the female during the part of the mating ritual when she is bitten by the male.

Nurse sharks performing their mating dance

REPRODUCTION

Sharks live solitary lives, coming together about once a year to mate. When females are ready to be courted, they send out strong chemicals that attract a male. Their courtship ritual involves swimming side by side, following each other's movements, and then moving to a more aggressive phase in which the male chases and bites the female. When the female agrees to mate, the male inserts one of his claspers, the long organs on his underside, into the female's cloaca, the opening on her underside, and fertilizes the eggs inside her.

Some shark species lay their eggs, and others carry their young—called pups—inside their bodies. Most sharks are ovoviviparous (oh-voh-vye-VIP-uh-riss). This means that after the eggs are fertilized, they develop and hatch inside the female, where the pups grow until they are born live. The pups first eat the yolk in the egg from which they hatch, but when that is gone, they eat their smaller brothers and sisters to survive until they are born. Most shark litters include between 4 and 20 pups.

SHARK
DANGER

Young sharks are often eaten by other sharks, crocodiles, seals, and big fish.

A newborn swell shark emerging from its egg sac

SHARK
GESTATION

The shortest known shark gestation period is five months (for the bonnethead shark). The spiny dogfish has the longest: 22 months.

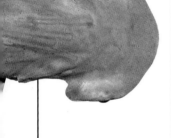

Above, the head of a bonnethead shark Right, the birth of a lemon shark pup, tail first

When the female shark is ready to give birth, she enters an estuary, a shallow, protected coastal area where river water mixes with seawater. As soon as the pups are born, she leaves them and swims back to sea. Since shark pups have such a long **gestation** period (9 to 12 months), they are able to swim and fend for themselves from birth. This is why the mother chooses a protected place to bear her young, and why estuaries are such an important part of the shark's habitat.

Sharks are slow to grow and develop. They live to be anywhere from 10 to 70 years old. Most are considered mature at 5 to 10 years of age.

As **top predators**, sharks have few natural enemies. Because of their size, speed, coloration, and other **adaptations**, not many animals can hurt them. Their main natural threats include larger sharks, killer whales, and humans. Of these enemies, humans pose by far the most dangerous threat.

Killer whales are one of the shark's few natural enemies

SHARK
DEFENSE

Sharks vomit as a means of self-defense. The cloud of vomited matter distracts or repels any creature harassing or threatening the shark.

SHARK
ATTACKS

Shark attacks kill fewer than 100 people each year. People, on the other hand, kill more than 100 million sharks each year.

23

SHARK

A very large great white shark will weigh a little more than 2,000 pounds (907 kg) and eat about 22,000 pounds (9,980 kg) of meat in one year.

A sucker on its head allows the remora to attach itself to a shark

On a smaller scale, sharks are bothered by copepods, small **crustaceans** that look like fleas. These **parasites** infest sharks' skin and the soft tissues of their eyes. Fortunately, sharks have a fish friend that can rid them of these pests. This fish, called a remora, has a sucker on top of its head, which it attaches to a shark. It then hitchhikes, using the shark's power to travel, and in exchange eats the copepods off the shark. This kind of relationship, in which two types of animals benefit from their interaction, is called mutualism.

Pilot fish often swim with sharks for protection from predators and to eat scraps from the sharks' meals.

25

Above, pilot fish using a shark for protection Left, a remora attached to a leopard shark

SHARK

F E A R

Because so many people misunder-stand the nature of sharks, many countries practice shark control, needlessly destroying sharks to protect people from shark attacks.

THE HUMAN THREAT

People have long killed sharks for meat, for medicine, for sport, and by accident. When fishing boats are out to catch a different fish and pull in a shark instead, the shark is often treated as bycatch (unwanted fish) and thrown back into the ocean after it has died. Some people practice finning, cutting off a shark's fin to sell for soup and leaving the injured shark to die. Every year, humans also kill many sharks to make medicines out of their cartilage and organs. Although scientific tests have not proven that these medicines work, many people believe in them and continue to buy them. All of these practices have caused a serious problem. Sharks reproduce and develop slowly, so when too many are killed, no younger sharks are born to take their place, and the shark population shrinks.

A whitetip reef shark

Only 30 shark species are truly dangerous to humans, and only five species are responsible for most attacks on humans. They are the great white, the tiger, the hammerhead, the bull, and the whitetip.

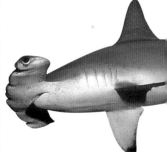

Environmental damage caused by humans also harms sharks. Much of the pollution that people allow to enter the ocean disrupts the fragile **ecosystems** of the estuaries that serve as shark nurseries. If sharks don't have safe places to reproduce and grow in their early years, the shark population will continue to shrink.

Above, a hammerhead shark
Left, a remora hitchhiking on a lemon shark

W hether human actions are intentional or accidental, the way we live often has a negative effect on the world of the shark. Because humans have generally feared sharks, it has taken a long time for us to recognize how seriously sharks are threatened. Several shark species will soon face **extinction** if nothing is done to change the human activities that harm them.

SHARK ATTACKS

Many attacks on humans occur because the shark mistakes the person for prey. For example, from below, scuba divers may look a lot like seals to a shark.

SHARK LEGENDS

Sharks appear in many legends from the Pacific Islands, sometimes as a devil or evil spirit, but more often as a god.

A whale shark surrounded by remoras and cobia

SHARK
A G E

*A shark's age can often be determined by examining its **vertebrae**. Sharks add one ring to their vertebrae each year. Counting the rings can determine the age of the shark.*

HELP FOR SHARKS

Scientists still have a lot to learn about sharks, and what they learn could be important for all humans. For example, sharks don't suffer from cancer or from many other diseases that humans do. This may mean that something in the shark's genetic make-up could tell us how to cure these diseases in humans. Keeping shark populations alive and growing is important if we hope to learn how they may help us one day.

But to save sharks from extinction, all of the world's countries will have to work together. The world's leaders should make finning illegal and limit the number of sharks a person can catch in a year. They should also limit the sale of sharks and shark products and create fishing nets that don't injure or accidentally trap sharks. More marine parks and sanctuaries would also help the sharks by providing protected areas for their young. Reducing pollution is important not only for sharks but for all animals—including humans—who rely on the ocean.

By taking small, simple actions—such as recycling, cutting down on pollution, and refusing to buy shark meat or products—we can all help keep sharks alive and swimming in the ocean.

SHARK
PRODUCTS

Shark skin has been used to decorate sword hilts and sheaths and was once used as sandpaper. Today, it is eaten in many Asian countries and used around the world to make shoes, belts, handbags, and wallets.

Whitetip reef sharks resting on the ocean floor

Glossary

Physical qualities that help plants or animals function in their environments are called **adaptations**. When an animal has one or more adaptations that allow it to survive in its environment, it is said to be well **adapted**.

Cartilage is an elastic tissue that makes up the skeleton of a shark. Human noses are also made of cartilage.

Shrimp, crabs, and lobsters are examples of **crustaceans**—animals that live in the water and have antennae, segmented legs, and mouths like jaws.

Ecosystems are made up of all the connected parts of a plant's or animal's environment. For example, water, fish, and plants are all parts of an ocean ecosystem.

Extinction is the elimination of a type of plant or animal from the planet. When the last plant or animal of a species dies, that species is extinct.

The period of time it takes for a fertilized egg to develop into an animal that's ready to be born is called **gestation**.

To **migrate** is to move from one area to another in order to feed or breed.

Parasites are creatures that live off of animals or plants of a different species and harm them.

Plankton are very small plants and animals that float in the ocean. They rely on the movement of the water for transportation, since they have no way to move themselves.

Predators are animals that kill and eat other animals.

A **species** is a closely related group of plants or animals that can breed with one another.

Animals that are **streamlined** have a body structure that allows them to move through water with little resistance.

Top predators are predators at the top of the food chain. Few, if any, other animals hunt or eat them. An animal that is hunted is called **prey**.

Vertebrae are the small, bony segments that make up an animal's spine.

Index